D1235932

Karyotype

Karyotype

Kim Trainor

Brick Books

Library and Archives Canada Cataloguing in Publication

Trainor, Kim, 1970–, author
        Karyotype / Kim Trainor.

Poems.
Issued in print and electronic formats.
ISBN 978-1-77131-379-7 (paperback).—ISBN 978-1-77131-381-0 (pdf).—
ISBN 978-1-77131-380-3 (epub)

        I. Title.

PS8639.R355K37 2015   C811'.6   C2015-903675-5
                                             C2015-903676-3

We acknowledge the Canada Council for the Arts, the Government of Canada
through the Canada Book Fund, and the Ontario Arts Council for their support of
our publishing program.

The author photograph was taken by Kristie Trainor.
The cover image is a photograph by Jeffery Newbury of the Beauty of Loulan.

The book is set in Adobe Garamond.
Cover design by Marijke Friesen.
Interior design and layout by Marijke Friesen.
Printed and bound by Sunville Printco Inc.

Brick Books
431 Boler Road, Box 20081
London, Ontario N6K 4G6

www.brickbooks.ca

for Madeleine, Finn, and Kieran

Table of Contents

I.

Karyotype

I

They peel her desiccated beauty—
soft-petalled husks of chestnut brown,
her skull in its silken pod—tease

open the parchment skin to flesh
stitched through with blue-dyed veins and pearls
of bone. What are they looking for

in their protection of white mask
and gown? I sit next to my daughter
who turns her face from their grim task

but I look, and my son looks too
into the Beauty of Loulan
preserved in our luminous blue

glass capsule, with all the others—
the Cherchen man, the toddler
with a flat stone on each eye,

the man sewn up with horsehair sutures
at his slender neck. Microscopic views:
white blood cells smeared across a slide

stained with Giemsa dyes, methylene blue
and azure A, B, C to show
the chromosomal bands of dark

and light. We watch this
in the dim twilight of our den,
my own small band of humans

eight, five, and not-quite-two,
transfixed by television's light
and incontrovertible skin.

Scientists now reach into her cavities,
extract woody shreds of dried leaves—
she has become leaf, pale flowers

interred. Pliny the Elder wrote
of "Serae" with flaxen hair and blue eyes
who made *an uncouth sort of noise*

by way of talking. We watch bright
threads of her DNA unwound
and read from left to right

and learn her history. But where is she,
in the blue-stained karyogram,
this desiccated woman

this Beauty of Loulan, this beauty?

II

Cold February world cracked open
this morning into particles,
quiet staccato of what remains

after winter's scouring tide: smudges
of pale green, the fuzzed almond
buds of star magnolia, snagged rosehips,

bruised and cauterized tabs of rotting
berries amongst delicate glass bulbs strung
in a bare tree, bright this dark morning.

Even the slender filaments
of crocuses like gas flames
rise out of the black earth. Now time

holds me, fettered to my young son.
He fills a rusted dump truck
with coarse grey sand. I watch, and think

in this excruciating limbo.
In this excruciating limbo
the sun cannot burn through the mist

of this grey morning. I watch him
fill his truck with handfuls of sand.
Dew lies on the grass. I watch him

and think how in my stillness
I've slipped through morning's deliquescence
and cyan skin to this still centre,

this thin band between earth and sky
like a clear glass slide
we stick to, and are translated.

I am threads unravelling, grains
of pollen sifted through small hands,
berries steeped in rain. Time

flows from us, unstanched, into the sand.

III

I lean towards microscopic views,
all the familiar words made strange
when mounted on slides we look right through

on the Kyowa Biolux-12.
Quick field notes jotted down
in a wilderness of language.

Onion rind peeled to a pale lilac
net of sheer elongated cells.
Fronds of disintegrating silk

slipped through the word. Surgical tubes
of nylon. Leaf spore resolved to annelids
and pressed sepia flowers

on an uncouth tongue. She is past
caring, her body now a manuscript
of faded letters and soft words

of mourning; comb and spindle,
whorl and winnowing tray, all her craft
long forgotten as she is left, thinned

to paper and clots of ink
that once ran clear in her, her life's
illumination, her life

resolved to heat-glazed onion skin,
to mute tendrils of kin.
I think I might be of her kind

deep in my own unconsecrated skin.

IV

He said that when he brought her from the grave
and held her in his arms, he thought, this beauty,
if she were alive today

or I three thousand years ago—
I would most certainly make her my wife.
And she—did she, so long ago

one morning, pick up her winnowing
tray, take handfuls of grain, and sing
of life long-flowing in her veins,

of each slow-shuttered cell of time
that held her in its arms or drew
the brown-dyed threads across her loom?

Did she hold a young son or daughter
with tender hands so beautiful
that now are splayed like whitened coral,

like sun-faded sea star or lily
dried to fragile tissue, so lithe,
so peaceful, as if life's tithe

yielded to desert sands? And did she
smooth the coarse brown cloth become her shroud
with slender fingers that could feel

fine bones slit through
her paper skin? This pale left hand
so delicately flexed, this limbo,

this warm salt current she's ever drifting through.

V

One cell of light this afternoon
in a grey season. Winter sun
grazes the pink seeping buds

of the flowering quince and the bare wood
of the hibiscus like an outstretched hand,
splintered fingers strung with glass beads

and suncatchers; light glints in shards,
flecks of sun cast to the black earth.
They could be artifacts, dense as words,

something you dig out of the ground,
that remembers human
work. For the precision of tendons

and sharp eyes and love, it all goes
to earth. As all through this winter day
the intermittent news

of a newborn found in Burns Bog.
He was wrapped in a towel at birth
and thrown away. Is there a myth

that can explain this suffering,
that can restore him,
or is it the usual story—

just one more sacrificial victim?

VI

Warm currents bring them to the surface
from time to time in fetal curls
like ammonites or scrolls

folded gently in
upon themselves, as if they held
unbearable secrets

that they must keep from harm
and yet unknown to their own selves.
See how they bear the plum-

dark burns where skin crisped and peeled
off the bone, and still visible
beneath, meticulous blue-inked

lines where the veins once ran through.
Here's one with arms held on by threads,
the eyes removed. Some sacrificed,

some drifting in a kind of peace,
all carry this scrolled secret
with a terrible grace

light as a fluttering silk ribbon,
what I would most know and not know
and carry all my life, though

dense and heavy as any stone.

VII

I listen for the rustling leaves
of the paper mulberry tree,
the delicate letters

dried to ash in the desert heat.
We sift them now for meaning,
our fingers black with it.

And the wet ink flowing through punctured
skin to lie along the cheek now cured
to leather. This has meaning too.

And deeper still tucked in the marrow
of each small fluted bone
a message in a foreign tongue

we struggle to decipher
with a rudimentary grammar
as if in its declensions we

could almost know what we once were.

VIII

I lie in a fetal curl
all night, drifting asleep to the drone
of helicopters slowly circling

this quiet rainforest city,
to spatters of rain on the glass.
And wake to drumming rain and darkness.

And drift away in rain and darkness.

IX

A cold Monday and we are here
again, at this park with the poured concrete
fossils, the furrowed trilobite

and horseshoe crab, its tail flicking
through currents of sand where the grazed
wings of a dragonfly lie scuffed

underfoot. Here we are again,
tracing our movements in the sand
dark silhouettes on metal rungs

pressed in clear time all morning long.

X

Another storm comes in tonight
off the Pacific. Thrum of rain
so insistent on the skylight's

resonant skin. It tamps me down
into the darkness of this night
till I am ossicles of sound,

small drops of swiftly falling rain.

XI

She takes in hand the shroud
of the blue-eyed boy and inspects
plain-woven woolen thread

of maroon and brown,
its only decoration
thin textured stripes of kinked-up

overspun yarn. There is a skill
to reading this faint signature
slipped through the cloth, subtle

indications of loom and mourning
in the small body so carefully
bound, in the small blue stones for eyes.

She pieces together his story
just as the blue felt cap was pressed
to his unfused skull and red wisps

of wool placed in each nostril
to stanch death's flow.
He is so gently swaddled

you could pick him up in your arms
and almost feel his breath,
you could cradle him in your arms

and feel his breath.

XII

Discs of thick coloured bottle glass
slotted in a cedar trellis
as we walk through morning sunlight

catch my eye. And further along,
a metallic wind chime
strung from the eaves, mustard and wine

in the shape of a parasol,
bright beads of light cast off each spoke.
I see the care that someone took

to collect these glass beads and chimes
in a clasp slender as the hand
of a child. Not a breath of wind

now, not a breath of wind this time.

XIII

This is the simplest kind of weave—
plain weave. The long warp threads are fixed
upon the loom, the mobile weft,

that which is woven, crosses
the warp at right angles, first under
then over, and at the line's end

a selvedge is quietly formed
like a scar, to stop the fleet unravelling
and open wound. So we are formed

along such ancient human drifting lines.

XIV

The image resolves to a line,
notched vertebrae, seed pearls
strung out along a spine

phosphorescent in the grey matrix.
Next to the first a second line
comes clear; they form a gentle helix

these two cleaved to one another
in the clay. Or is it a wisp
of thread torn from a woven cloth,

the weft still taut across the warp,
the pattern that tells a story
still clear and sharp?

It can happen this way.
We lay our fine bones down into the clay
in the cold dark

and tender ourselves in threads of DNA.

XV

Green shoots poke through
the mud, past an armature of branches
flecked with berries and pewter

drops of rain, cells clasped in a pellucid
skin my son plucks with small fingers,
the light running clear.

He plucks them gently and the light runs clear.

XVI

Running the length of the skinny
little body, the narrow cloth
is wrapped, the tan warp tucked across

her like the threads of a cocoon,
as she is waiting to emerge
from her long sleep. Moon-

face in her pod of softest brown
stitched closed with carved bone pins,
the mottled wasp-nest skull

and tapered form
so carefully framed with selvedges
and checks, as though a young woman

had made this as she learned to weave,
a sampler gangly as the child
she had to wrap so carefully and leave

in the cold ground, her child.

XVII

I turn the pages of the book
with diagrams in black and white
of different kinds of weave, dialects

of Tokharian, the small tongue
tamped in the mouth of a newborn human.
I feel the weight of my own skull

thick with flu, the hollows, the thin tubes
of blood and clear fluid that run
quick through channels along the bone.

Shuttered views of a felt hood
shaped at the crown by heavy stitches,
cross-sections of a grave. I feel it

working its way out beneath my skin
like a crocus bulb in this early spring,
bone petals just below the surface

yearning for sun.

XVIII

Sunk in this cave, the chalk-white sockets
my eyes look through, seared cheek bones,
the mouth's damp wound.

Through the slant golden light
their voices come from the school ground.
Resonant bone.

Drifting, pure sound.

XIX

A word tries to work its way through
her mouth dried wide open in death,
past the circlet of broken teeth

and the swollen tongue that filled the gap
in her dried seed head.
But she is all stitched up—

her lips fine strings that draw her taut,
her skin still delicate
tapestry of threaded gold,

finely lashed seams that close each lid
and braids that bind her skull.
Only the dark red chin strap failed

to hold her closed, so her mouth gapes
in death. And I would hold it closed
for her, and gently seal her lips

but for this word she'll never speak.

XX

The window is scored
with arterial branches drawn
this overcast morning

black as the inked words I scratch out
in my notebook. Across the street
beneath the dripping chestnut trees

silver discs glitter in the field,
the school ground strewn with puddles,
shards excavated

at recess among cut hawthorn
and channels dug in the sand.
I score a line and start again.

Chiselling out the word's thin form
just glimpsed in the strata of language,
small cuts that try to gauge

the spine's articulations
and the ungainly head.
Clearing the fine dust with my breath

until it begins to emerge—
the outline coming clear
from salt-white paper.

A fossil embryo. A word.

XXI

Now the trees rise out of the dusk,
out of the mud and silver
as the heavy rain lets up,

scorched coral rising
from wet clay,
lithe fingers splayed

across the sky.

XXII

The crocuses that were stiff blue flames
are broken now, their wrung necks
laid on banks of moss. All the same.

Life furls somewhere below.
I lie with them in pearls of bone,
in dark earth that shudders faintly

without a sound.

XXIII

I peel back ivory leaves,
bone petals, to the bruised image
of this Beauty

of Loulan. Furred chrysalis
on white enamel,
handful of dried leaves.

Her scorched face slips through
the split chestnut hood
and cusp of fur.

Twig legs pierce the split husk
of her. She is becoming new,
some other thing that moves through

what she once was. I study her
closely through the long afternoon
as the rain pours down,

glancing up to trees skinned with moss
in the green flickering gloom,
a castle's ruins strewn

across the living room floor.
But always back to her dark form.
What am I looking for

in her slim body like a root
or iris corm
that carries tamped within

a genetic script of unfurling blue?
There is no sequence
that can describe her.

No karyogram
to take the imprint
of this woman.

But still we scrape off letters
from her parchment skin,
which she endures,

the chrysalis
scored and split
as she rises

from the page
leaving only a drop of ink
and the discarded husk

of her skin.

II.

On the ordering of chaotic bodies of poetry

1.

Ovid knew about this—

spilt blood of Adonis
to stanch the anemone's
pale throat

a tongueless woman
hatched into a bird
takes flight.

2.

And Callimachus
after the ink had bled
into the cracks in his fingers
the cross-hatched fibres
of his skin

his catalogue complete—

could he still hear
in the rustle of papyrus
their clamorous voices
rising above the lyre?

3.

"Aristophanes [of Byzantium] arranged the Pindaric corpus into seventeen books: hymns and paeans in one book each; dithyrambs, processionals, maiden songs, and poems for dancing in two books each (with perhaps an added book for purely secular maiden songs); four books of victory songs; and a book each of encomia and threnoi."

—*W. R. Johnson,* The Idea of Lyric

He performs a careful anatomy—
amygdala, vitreous, heart

every organ observed

the spinal column opened

to reveal the twined sinews
the fascicles of nerves

before fluids pool and obscure.

4.

So much more orderly than Sappho, strips of lyric used to line sarcophagi, lovers' words poured into desert sands.

We scour the rubbish tips at Oxyrhynchus for her remains.

5.

I can hear their voices. Like a fine whisper of rain coming over the field. I read late into the night:

"14 March 1917. Ronville O.P. Looking out towards No Man's Land what I thought first was a piece of burnt paper or something turned out to be a bat shaken at last by shells from one of the last sheds in Ronville . . ."

—from the war diary of Edward Thomas

6.

Their whispers in the archives:

"A small Walker's Back-Loop pocket-book bound in pigskin and priced at two shillings. The covers and the pages are concaved and creased suggesting that he was carrying the diary when he was killed at an observation post on the 9th April 1917 by a shell blast during the opening barrages of the Battle of Arras."

—archival description of the diary of Edward Thomas

7.

Stitch the torn spine closed
with quiet words

and lines of moving
light and shadow.

Smooth the creased skin
over bone-white

pages and clean
the concaved wounds

with cherry petals
soaked in rainwater.

8.

Nadezhda Mandelstam hid her husband's poems in cushions and saucepans,
kettles and baskets and shoes, interleaved in the pages of her dissertation on
linguistics. And when the *idyllic era of cushions* had passed—she hid them in
memory, as she worked nights at the textile factory in Strunino.

9.

Samizdat blooming like gilia after desert rains.

10.

And this one too:

"A visiting card with the name Dr. Miklós Radnóti printed on it. An ID card stating the mother's name as Ilona Grosz. Father's name illegible. Born in Budapest, May 5, 1909. Cause of death: shot in the nape. In the back pocket of the trousers a small notebook was found soaked in the fluids of the body and blackened by wet earth. This was cleaned and dried in the sun."

—Coroner's Report on Corpse No. 12, exhumed from a mass grave in the village of Abda, Hungary, at the end of the Second World War

11.

Take this fluid-seeped
notebook in your hands.

See where the ink blooms
and clots on the page

this tissue-thin poppy
risen from wet earth

cleaned and dried in the sun.

12.

The gracile fascicles
carrying fine shivers

to her brain as she stitched
each poem into its booklet.

13.

A return to biology. Poems slotted into kingdom, genus, species. Sliced and stained with methylene blue and mounted on a slide.

A taxonomy.

A poem laboratory.

14.

Japanese Stab Binding. Ethiopian. Coptic. Stitched. Glued.

These are the principal kinds of binding.

15.

A.W. Lewis (1957) recommends the following tools:

bone folder, glue kettle, needles, brushes, hammer, and tenon saw
a good sharp penknife, a paring knife and strop, an awl
sewing frame, nipping press, standing press, lying press, and plough.

16.

I hear their voices when the rain falls and chestnuts clatter on the roof, their clamour as the corms and roots and seeds rot in wet earth.

17.

And then there was Liu Baiqiang
sentenced to eighteen years for "Counter-Revolutionary Incitement"
who attached words to the legs of locusts

Tyranny!   *Long Live Freedom!*

and flung them over the walls
of his prison, into the air.

Oxyrhynchus

They use x-rays now
and infrared

to read the faded ink
on papyri fragments

the ancient words
coming clear

the coursing blood
beneath the skin.

The semantic fields of glass and other transparent materials in the poetry of Krzysztof Kamil Baczyński

> ...*in her body of glass*
> *she pours silver droplets of speech.*
> —"Biała Magia" ("White Magic")

In which a poem is:

1. A lens to focus sunlight, to magnify the world. (Blackened ribs.)

2. A glass shard lodged in the eye. (Men like burnt cinders.)

3. Fields of ice. (Wires. Roots. Rubble. Tanks. Strata of human dead.)

4. A man. (A page clotted with words. Iron arms. Charred heart.)

5. A woman. (The dark embryo. Shrapnel. Maggots. Grass.)

Field notes: Arras 1917

I reach for you in the dark.
Tap of rain on the skylight.
My fingers graze concaved skin
drawn over chiselled spine.

You are hollowed out
like the bones of hedge-sparrows
and larks and chinking blackbirds.

No man's land is written over
in your cramped hand.
The enemy's plane is a pale moth
amongst shrapnel bursts.
Shells into Beaurains all night
like starlings coming home.
Your orchard dugout
is fledged with yarrow
and any day now you will take
the old grey-green track
that silvers no man's land,
the old country way to Arras.

*

Artillery wakes me,
a shell-burst of lightning
and the drag of thunder.
The night flaps like a great sail

(in the chrysalis of sleep rain falls
on the blackened arms
of the quince, gashed
with small petalled mouths
and skinned with green).

*

At dusk the magnolia blooms
are strung on bare wood

like paper lanterns
across the bruised sky

or the clothes women hang to dry
on barbed entanglements.

*

My son comes to me
when I'm reading, takes out
the Monarch butterfly
he brought home crumpled
in his pocket.

Its papery wings lift
with our breath.

When I return to my book
dried glue sifts down its spine
into my cupped hand.

*

Your youngest daughter wrote
that the pages of your diary
were curiously ridged
like the scallops of a seashell.

This Walker's Back-Loop pocket-book
carries the only mark of your death.

I don't understand
why you went to France.

       *

In my dream
where there is no song
no lark or thrush
I bring to your grave
a bleached snail shell
and the roots
of a wild cherry.

Russian notebook: Moscow 1918–1920

At 10 o'clock the day is over. Sometimes I chop and saw wood for tomorrow. At 11 or 12 I am also in bed. Happy with the lamp right next to my pillow, the silence, a notebook, a cigarette, and sometimes—bread.
        —Marina Tsvetaeva, notebook entry, Moscow 1919

Telegraph lines the words sing down
at the speed of light, an open vein—

            *

Moscow, November 1919. See her, there, waking in grey light in the attic room of her former house to split wood and start the fire. She is alone in revolutionary Moscow with two young girls to care for. Potatoes boil in the samovar she stokes with coals. Her brown flannel dress singed by flakes of ash and cigarettes. Fingerless mittens. Donated lunch tickets—everyone afraid for her and her children. So impractical. A copper mess kit and a milk can to collect the free meals from Prechistenka street. House key strung around her neck. The cold. Banisters and attic beams chopped up for fuel. *The exhilaration.*

            *

On a trip to Tamvor guberniya
to "study" handmade embroidery
she barters matches, soap, and chintz
(really, rose-coloured damask) for:

18 pounds of wheat
10 pounds of flour
3 pounds of lard
3 wooden dolls and a necklace
of dark amber beads, which you cannot eat.

            *

(Her first daughter, Ariadna—Alya—is born in 1912. By 1919 she is already writing poems.)

*

Tough arteries, thick tubes flush with life.
Thin veins of dark red blood that seek the heart.

*

Moscow, November 1918. Narkomnats (People's Commissariat of Nationalities), Information Section, in the "Rostovs' house" from *War and Peace*. Open the door, just a glimpse: pink walls and desk under chandeliers. Her third day on the job. She is compiling a newspaper archive that no one will read. She paraphrases reports of prisoners of war, the movements of the Red Army, the White Guard, advances, retreats, all copied onto cards. The clippings are pasted onto sheets she captions in lilac pencil. When some clippings are lost, she makes them up.

*

There are lines for everything

a line for milk on Kudrinskaya street
a line for salted fish on Povarskaya
a line for hemp-seed oil on the Arbat

a line into the cellar for half-thawed, half-rotten potatoes
she pulls home on Alya's sled
with blue reins and bells

blue-shadowed line the runner carves in snow.

*

(Her second daughter, Irina, is born in 1917. There is something wrong. At two and a half she can barely walk or speak. *But she can sing.*)

*

Moscow, November 1919. Lunch ticket, milk can, copper mess kit. She takes Alya with her to collect the meal. Ties Irina to a chair so that she won't get into trouble while they're gone.

*

A line of hunger (of indifference? desperation?)
the length of a cord that ties a child to a chair.

*

Moscow, December 1919. She places Alya and Irina in the Kuntsevo orphanage with the hope they can feed her daughters through the winter.

*

She takes refuge in the shelter of the line,
its cadences, its nooks and crevices.

*

"Represented on a graph, Tsvetaeva's work would exhibit a curve—or rather, a straight line—rising at almost a right angle because of her constant effort to raise the pitch a note higher, an idea higher (or, more precisely, an octave and a faith higher). She always carried everything she has to say to its conceivable and expressible end."

—*Joseph Brodsky*

*

45

"Poems are the tracks by which I enter your soul. But your soul recedes and I get impatient, I jump ahead, blindly on the off chance, and then I wait in trepidation: will it turn my way?"

— Tsvetaeva, letter to Pasternak

*

Lines jump the poem's tracks
pitched onto the walls of her room.

*

Moscow, January 1920. She finds Alya deathly ill at the orphanage and brings her home on a borrowed sledge.

*

Poetry is language pared to the line,
flesh almost to the bone.

*

Moscow, February 1920. Irina dies of starvation in the Kuntsevo orphanage. Two years and seven months old.

*

The line of a neck slender
as a dandelion stem.

*

Moscow, February 1920. One last glimpse. Midnight.
The lamp drawn close. The notebook closed.

Look away.

See the stain of words on the shadowed walls.

Russian notebook: Voronezh 1935–1937

I have often been asked about the origin of these "Notebooks." This was the name we used to refer to all the poems composed between 1930 and 1937 which we copied down in Voronezh in ordinary school exercise books (we were never able to get decent paper, and even these exercise books were hard to come by)...
　　—Nadezhda Mandelstam, *Hope Against Hope*

Two elements:

Black Earth. Chernozem of the steppe—
furrows planted with seed, little bones.

Air. Vault of stars and rushing signals—
from static tune the chirrups, longings, hums.

*

In exile in Voronezh, after living for a time in a glassed-in veranda, they rented a room in the house of an agronomist who wore high leather boots. They disappointed him: *I thought you'd have writers like Kretova and Zadonski coming to see you, and we'd all be dancing the rumba together.*

*

In exile in Voronezh, where the ice forms a skin of glass, he began to write the poem he hoped would save his life.

*

Black earth that receives
all bodies, cracked flute

of the spine, crushed trachea

the breath of the steppe
whispers through.

*

The archive: three notebooks, school exercise books, in which she recorded
his poems in violet ink (ink splatters, splash of a comet's tail, liquid trace of a
voice). Then he would write the date and a *V* next to this, like a brand.

*

Today, as I write of Voronezh of seventy years ago, a snow of fine glass seeds falls
on the crocuses and moss in this rainforest on the north Pacific. It makes a faint
sound, a metallic shiver, needles on glass.

*

The first Voronezh notebook: Spring, 1936. Twenty-two poems. He is coming
to terms with the black earth.

*

And here he gives voice to the *whispering "cat language"*—k, p, t, ch—*of
Armenian*....

*

After years practicing the *genre of silence.*

*

At the same time as he is serving his three-year exile in Voronezh, his namesake is lecturing in Moscow on the way light scatters on thermal acoustic waves. He incorporates the language of quantum physics into his poem on the unknown soldier, a lament for the victims of the purges and all the future dead, towards whom threat travels at the speed of light.

*

At midnight he listens
to his crystal set
which consists of:

earphones

an antenna

a thin sharp wire called a "cat's whisker"
which is drawn over a crystal
(galena, for example)
to search for points of reception
faint scratch of static ...

... the Spasskaya Tower Clock on Red Square
chimes in the small bones of his ear
and travels down his long frame
to the receiving earth.
That little irony—*naushniki,*
"earphones"—the same word for
"informer."

*

The second Voronezh notebook: Winter, 1937. Forty-five poems. Including one which describes Stalin as an idol in a cave, trying to recall his human form.

*

Improvised crystals—

rusted pennies
pencil lead
a blue steel razor
a human skull.

*

The transcriptions of his poems are shadows,
cardiographs, brittle score of his voice.

*

And Voronezh, sealed under glass,
a social experiment mounted on a slide.

*

He sounds Keats' flutes and urns, the poetic
spirit that breathes through vessels of clay.

*

Cracked, fluted bone
resonant hums, sudden

interruption of breath—
all the stops—

tamped in black earth.

*

The third Voronezh notebook: Spring, 1937.
Twenty-two poems. There is so little time.

*

"If people could hear his voice, they would understand what he meant by 'in-
terpretive reading'—that is, using the text as a conductor uses a score. This
could never be properly conveyed by some form of phonetic notation showing
where he paused or raised his voice. His treatment of vowel quantity and the
timbre of his voice could not be indicated. And what memory could ever pre-
serve all the inflections of a voice that fell silent a quarter of a century ago? Yet
something of his voice is preserved in the very structure of his verse. Nothing
can be completely scattered to the winds."

—*Nadezhda Mandelstam,* Hope Against Hope

*

But so many are. The ones we will never hear.

*

The breath of the steppe whispers through.

*

Night falls
on the Pacific
and the snow falls,
softly,
in the blue night.

"In the long hours of darkness, Baghdad shakes to the constant low rumble of B-52s"

In a hotel room by the Tigris a man writes.
A jar with a clutch of flowers trembles
on the windowsill as the air pressure drops,
while out in the desert
soldiers hide in furrows of night.
A pale red stain appears—
its penumbra blooms
and is extinguished.
The man writes about the war,
about the smell of burnt flesh
along the road north of Nasiriyah,
about this dark sound.
The air pressure drops again. A tremor
runs through the water in the jar,
the thin stalks, the petals.

Membrane of ice on the windows of this room in Montreal.
I cup my hands, peer into the television's blue cave, and see
pale slivers of tracer fire in the desert,
missiles scattered like black seeds,
a pale red stain on the horizon that pours back into the dark.
Through a live street cam, somewhere in Baghdad,
the shadows of men. I can hear them—
they call to one another in their language,
and at dawn, the birds sing.

Poem from a burnt notebook

The taste of smoke and poems
Written by my hand...
    — Anna Akhmatova, "Sweetbrier in Blossom"

I.

Call them "ashtray poems," these poems
scribbled on paper, quickly memorized
beneath bright, empty chatter, then
the rasp and flare of a match.

                    Now comes
the charred taste of words.
The crisp blackened skin.
Gleam of white scapula.
Only the voice survives
this *beautiful and mournful ritual.*

II.

She burned her archive
three times—
scraps of paper torn
from school copy books,
poems on the verso
of Mandelstam's drafts, thin sheets
his words bled through.

Her voice caught, snagged
on black Cyrillic.

Her voice alight
at the rasp of a match,
blue smoke and
rendered ash.

III.

This morning, snow
thin as paper
on frozen ground.

I carry her poems
in my hand.
              Scatter them.

Words hop like sparrows—
a softness, a handful of little bones.

They alight
on the bright red drops
of Japanese barberry,
its weeping thorns.

Ash

For example, when Serbian nationalists in the hills circling Sarajevo
firebombed the National and University Library of Bosnia and Herzegovina
1.5 million books burned
including the card catalogues, all bibliographic trace
including the archives of the Serbian poet Aleksa Šantić
and the Croatian poet Silvije Strahimir Kranjčević.

A few books were saved, carried by hand, and a few,
the sun veiled in a pall of grey from their burning,
could still be read one last time as pages floated down,
black letters burning on grey.

                              You could, it is said,
catch them in your hand like snowflakes
and read the words as they melted to ash.

III.

How to make a human karyotype

1

Draw 10 mL of venous blood. Follow the protocols for lymphocyte separation and inoculation and the incubation of cultures.

From a height of several feet release a drop of cell suspension onto a slide soaked overnight in absolute methanol.

Hold over an open flame to burn away the fixative.

Submerge in Giemsa stain, then view through a light microscope these banded chromosomes you will cut out and arrange into Rorschach blots, fingers of desiccated coral.

2

Anoint your newborn's crumpled palms and fingers
with some blue pigment, then gently press
to a square of unmarked paper each small hand.

3

Write one word after another
and then another, these stitches of ink,
these seams of fractured light.

Cradle song: Six variations

1.

The rain pools
in your small skull,
so new it gapes
in its dressing
of pale skin, collects
this quiet sound.

Here you shelter
in its cracked hollow
sutured with blue
threads and gauze,
hematite stains
on the walls,
as if in the caves
of Laas Ga'al,
of Niaux.

2.

A synapse flares
down Neanderthal lines—
a handprint,
a horse outflung—
then dies, guttering
into shadow.

Down it comes
drumming, drumming,
races the tide.

3.

Listen—
the blood's hush
and sluice through
channels wormed
in bone. The sea
rushes in, spill
of sound over
lip and drum.

Rushes out
in sighs and whispers
through little holes.

4.

These holes I finger,
place my mouth
to your ocarina skull.

5.

And what thin wires
attached at temple and wrist
play your startles
and grimaces,
vacant smiles,
marionette frowns—
these life throes?

6.

Then let go
as you slip away,
your fuzzed head
on my collar bone
like the blueish bud
of a poppy, sodden
with drumming rain.

Hush, hush. Listen
to its song, gentle
sluice of drumming rain.

Blue-eyed boy

A smooth, curved slab of wood gave first notice of its presence. Underneath the slab, a
small secondary pit held a tiny, perfectly preserved baby.
> —Elizabeth Wayland Barber, *The Mummies of Ürümchi*

I

The grave lay beneath a slab of hollowed-out poplar
and a thick layer of reed mats, a "small secondary pit"
identified as Tomb 1, because they found it first;
it must have been added after the main burial
of three women and a man. (One of the women
might have been the mother, but this is speculation.)
The child, about three months old, had been placed there
on a white felt blanket. A second, whiter blanket
of long-hop twill folded over raw wool served as a pillow
for its head. The child had been wrapped in a purplish-red shroud
bound with twisted cords of red and blue.
"Two small bluish stones still close the infant's eyes."
A tradition of placing coins on eyes in Central Asia
can be traced back at least as far as the Parthians.
Tufts of wool in each nostril wicked away decomposition fluids.
Its features, its nose and eyebrows, are perfectly preserved.
A blue cap of barely felted wool and an edging of red
has been placed over the head with its wisps of pale brown hair.
Beside it were found a small cow's horn drinking cup
and a primitive baby bottle made from a sewn sheep's udder;
it still preserved some milk solids.

2

                              I have tried only
to describe this burial site as precisely as I can.
No metaphor can transform death or grief.
These are the grave goods that were found.
This is the body of the child.
This all happened a long time ago.

3

No, no—this isn't what I meant to write.
Tear out your hair and rend your flesh, anything
to mourn the life of this child.

Lines on a Cherchen grave

A line of cerulean blue seals in the heat of this dry land.
Here the sands of the Taklamakan fill a wide-mouthed shallow basin
high on a plateau nicknamed *Tuzluqqash,* which is Uyghur for "salt rock,"
the salt a metre thick, so pure the locals come to salvage it,
and some come also to dig in these sands for grave goods, all the remnants
strewn up there on the surface because they never find much of value
in this dry sand (*two drinking horns*) glittering with salt (*a sheep's head*).
Here some loose reeds are spread (*a saddle*) (*a small clay jar*), a scattering
of reeds that release a faint sickly-sweet scent as they are exposed
to the air (*a white felt blanket*) (*a brown kaftan*) for the first time
in three thousand years. Dust motes ride in the light. Which soon gives way
to a nest of braided mats neatly plaited as a woman's hair.
A rank softness of wild horse and cured buffalo skins drawn taut on
this lattice of bound twigs and timber beams—see how it is suspended
over a space of air and dark.

Sunlight breaks through here.

Sifting fingers
of light that stop (*a woman on her side, badly decomposed*), stop—
and then move on (*a man, ochre spirals at each temple*) and rest
for just a moment (*two small bone spoons and a dish of ochre pigment*)
on pale willow mats that serve for a floor (*two women, side by side*).

Under this—the indiscriminate earthen dark.

Tokharian love song

Purely secular "literature" has so far found but a single text...
—J. P. Mallory and Victor H. Mair, *The Tarim Mummies*

No one dearer than you.
No one dearer than you,
    never another.
My love for you is breath,
is life. There is no other.

I used to think like this:
My love, my life, will last—
    this was my thought.
A love without deceit,
God alone knew my thought.

He led you away therefore,
took this heart that was yours
    to my sorrow.
He tore your heart from me
and left me sorrow.

That which is woven

I'm reading about the Qäwrighul child
this afternoon, in November sunlight—
a clear cold light, the blue sky stained with ochre,
leaves strewing the ground.
                          There's a photograph
of this eight-year-old child swaddled in cloth
that has been closed with wooden pegs, like stitches
that hold together the lip of a wound,
and another that shows the complicated
pattern of the cloth: a tight checkerboard
of chestnut and tan, slashes of white weft
like keloid scars, thin stripes of oatmeal, tea,
scraped patches.
                 Transitions are "inexperienced,
haphazard"—see how strange, the uneven
zones of colour and different weaves—"but that
is how one learns." There is no symmetry
on any axis.
             I learn what I can
and think about setting up the warp threads
on a loom, try out foreign words, like *weft*
and *shuttle*, weave a mottled stripe of words
along the papery skull of the child.

But the child—someone bound so carefully
its skinny body with this cloth, it carries
the memories of her fingers, her loss.
Her love is crookedly stitched into this shroud.

I can see it clearly as the weak sun
of this November afternoon, oblique
through dying leaves, spins threads of gold,
thin bands of golden weft that touch these lines,
my threadbare offering.

Funeral rites

The forensic scientists have laid out the "Beauty of Krorän" on their dissecting table…
—J. P. Mallory and Victor H. Mair, *The Tarim Mummies*

Turn the page and she is there—

the Beauty of Loulan, or more correctly, Krorän, from the medieval Chinese *glu-glân* or *lɔu-lan*, a corruption of *kru-ran*. Known to the Uyghurs as Kirurän Guzäli, the Beauty of Krorän.

We call her the Beauty of Loulan because we do not know her name.

In Xinjiang, near Loulan, along the old Silk Road, on the northern tip of Lop Nor, in the sand, where her people placed her in a shallow grave.

We know she suffered. Scientists place her on the dissecting table as on an altar, her desiccated frame light as paper. She snaps like twigs. For a long time in silence they study her cured blackened body.

And when they had held her and mourned her they dressed her in a felted hood and a knee-length wrap which they secured with a wooden pin, and they laid her in the sand, in the shallow grave, and placed a winnowing basket across her face, then bundles of sticks and twigs, then layers of reeds, then a layer of branches again and so they returned her to the Taklamakan.

They study her hood. It is made of felted wool and dark brown woven cloth, which she might have stitched with her own hands. Stitches that run from the forehead across the pieces of felt and woven cloth that had been molded to her skull. A tall feather sticks out the top. One of them notes, in this hood and wrap secured with a wooden pin she looks like a girl playing "Indians."

And they buried her with a small comb which had four teeth missing and a neatly woven bag with some grains of wheat inside, and a large winnowing basket placed over her face and breast.

"Provision against the cold winter clearly concerned her; perhaps she died in the winter."

And they anointed her with ochre and they placed her in the grave.

"She is no longer articulate." But meaning can always be teased from the dead.

And they left her in the shallow grave and they turned away.

At the Shanghai Institute of Blood Transfusion they take a bone relic, a strand of auburn hair and determine that she had Type O blood. Now they study her mitochondrial DNA.

For four thousand years she remained in her grave.

She suffered. Head and pubic lice. Nits clustered at the base of eyelashes and brows. She breathed in charcoal and silicate dust from windblown sands and indoor fires that blackened her lungs. The remains of one bed bug, *Cimex centicularis*, were found on her body. She measured five feet two inches tall. She was forty years old.

Her twig legs poke out from her fur-lined skirt. Bone splits the skin. I want to cradle her in my arms and gently place her in her grave.

I will lie beside her one day.

Turn the page and she is there—

Papery chrysalis in a dish of white enamel.

Dried leaf that crumbles in your fingers.

Chaff.

IV. Nothing is lost

Through tools and acts of making, human beings become implicated in each other's sentience. Seeing is seeing of x, *and the one who has made the* "x" *has entered into the interior of the other person's seeing, entered there in the object of perception. The objects of hearing, desire, hunger, touch, are not just passively grasped by the fixed intentional states: the objects themselves act on the state, sometimes initiating the state, sometimes modifying it, increasing, decreasing, or eliminating it. Thus when intentional objects come to include not just the rain, berries, stones, and the night but also bread, bowls, church steeples, and radiators, there comes to be an ongoing interaction at the (once private) center of human sentience; for not only are the interior facts of sentience projected outward into the artifact in the moment of its making, but conversely those artifacts now enter the interior of other persons as the content of perception and emotion. Thus in the transformation of a weapon into a tool, everything is gained and nothing is lost.*

—Elaine Scarry, *The Body in Pain: The Making and Unmaking of the World*

In the six weeks since the ICRC *published its second 'Book of Belongings', containing photographs of possessions found with mortal remains around Srebrenica, in eastern Bosnia-Herzegovina, the book has been consulted by more than 1,600 persons looking for their missing loved ones.*

The publication contains 2,702 photos of clothes, jewellery and other personal effects found on the exhumed bodies of persons who disappeared when the town was overrun in July 1995. The photos relate to 473 cases of unidentified remains, and are in addition to the 1,756 photos published by the ICRC *last June in a book that also related to the Srebrenica missing.*

To date, 139 objects, concerning 64 cases, have been recognized in the new book. On this basis, forensic experts from the Podrinje Identification Project in Tuzla, which is part of the Missing Persons Institute, will start the procedure of identifying the remains.

—05-07-2001 News Release by the International Committee of the Red Cross

a list of artifacts that can be worn or carried
a loss that cannot be recorded in many pages
a notebook cleaned and dried in the sun
along the edges of the field, in streams and gutters
an archaeology of DNA and scarce belongings
annotations in the margins
are in addition to the 1,756 photos published by the ICRC
artifact in the moment of its making

become implicated in each other's sentience
belonged to a woman, this bracelet bright along the bone
belonging as sinew and syntax
'Book of Belongings' containing photographs of possessions
bowls, church steeples, and radiators, there comes to be an ongoing interaction
bring her out of the earth
bring him into the sun
bring them

carried in the pockets of her winter coat, sea glass and stones
carried out of the earth like a child
carry him in your arms, bring her into the sun
cases of unidentified remains are in addition to the 1,756 photographs
clay sticks to hem of coat and sleeves
close eyes, close mouth
closed with quiet words
clothed in a language that cannot stretch so thin

desire, hunger, touch, are not just passively grasped
diary that records the small hours
disappeared when the town was overrun in July 1995
drawn in blue-black ink
drawn on paper that can remember the precise locations
drawn out over years that are endured
dried in the sun
dried out sticks of words

earth of roots, seeds, seepage, litter, eyeglass
elements oxygen carbon hydrogen nitrogen calcium
enter the interior of other persons as the content of perception and emotion
entered there in the object of perception
entered there where it must be written
even a scrap of cloth or DNA as record
every word collected
everything is gained and nothing is lost

facts of sentience projected outward into the artifact
fingers of light sifting the leaves
floral print of a scarf, stitched ox-eye, violet, wild carrot
flowering that comes in the spring
flowers that are mostly small and white
forensic experts from the Podrinje Identification Project in Tuzla
found in several locations
found in the cracks, these small white flowers

gained and nothing is lost
gesture of a hand in conversation
glint of tools at dusk
glove with traces of dirt, spores, clay, blood
grammar to join the scattered words
grave where you scatter seeds
grow wildflowers
grows dark

has entered into the interior of the other person's seeing
hat drawn over contours of hair, skin, bone threaded with vein
hat lined with felt for warmth
having small stitches
here a hand laboured
here in this earth
hundreds of artifacts worn and carried
husks

I was this one and no other
identity card with name and photograph and number
in memory where the timbre of a voice is held
in search of what has been taken
in the moment of its making with loom, press, spool, thread
ink blooms and clots on the page
interior facts of sentience projected outward into the artifact in the moment
    of its making
interior of other persons as the content of perception and emotion

jar of small white flowers
jewelled beads of rain
jewellery, and other personal effects found on the exhumed bodies
join beads, shards, words as they slot together
join stems, join leaves
journey to these precise locations
just as it was, before
just the rain, berries, stones, and the night

keep looking
kept in a pocket
key to open a door
keyed to sorrow
kin drawn from marrow
kindling of the small wrist bones
kindness where it is found
known as this one and no other

labour recalled in each join, seam, stitch
language pared to the line
lattice of ribs
letter with news from a daughter
list of belongings
lithium strontium aluminum silicon lead
looking for their missing loved ones
lore of those who are missing, that they will one day be found

made of sand, lime, and soda ash
marble with a twist of colour, kept in a pocket
marked with scuffs and scratches
materials of earth
minutes counted
molybdenum fluorine chlorine iodine
moment of its making
more than 1,600 persons looking for their missing loved ones

name inscribed in a notebook
never meet on this earth
non omnis moriar
not alone
not just the rain, berries, stones, and the night
notebook cleaned and dried in the sun
notes in blue-black ink
nothing is lost

of those who are missing
offering of words
on this earth
ordered rows
other person's seeing entered there
oval buttons sewn by hand
over now
overrun in July 1995

pages of photographs
persons as the content of perception and emotion
persons looking for their missing loved ones
phosphorescence you lifted from the sea in strings of light
phosphorus potassium sulfur sodium magnesium
photograph of a woman on the shore
protocols for lymphocyte separation and inoculation
published its second 'Book of Belongings'

quadratic equation written on a scrap of paper
quarrel that will never end
quell hope, quell sorrow
query sent on official paper
quest for those who are missing
questions you keep asking
quiet as breath
quietness

rain, berries, stones, and the night
rain that began to fall when we first met
related to the Srebrenica missing
ring engraved with initials
risen from wet earth
rituals to join together and to release the dead
roots grow
rots now

saturated ground
second 'Book of Belongings,' containing photographs of possessions
seeing is seeing of x
sentience projected outward into the artifact in the moment of its making
shoe with traces of mud and clay
signs in the broken earth, the scattering of leaves
silence when we once talked
silent, this night

t-shirt put on without thought one morning
taken without warning
tell me how it was when we first met
the last time I saw you
the rain, berries, stones, and the night
to date, 139 objects, concerning 64 cases, have been recognized in the new book
to join together and to release the dead
transformation of a weapon into a tool, everything is gained and nothing is lost

umbrella with torn skin
under a deluge of rain, the muddy field
under the belief they will one day be found
understand that you are not forgotten
unidentified remains, and are in addition to the 1,756 photos published
unless you come to me in a dream
until I come to you
until then

vacant field
vastness of time
vein of words chiselled out
vest made of cotton
view of dried grasses and wildflowers, the horizon's blue line
vigil at dusk
vigilance
voice heard at the edges of sleep

we shall never meet again in this world
weapon into a tool, everything is gained and nothing is lost
where they will be found
which is part of the Missing Person's Institute, will start the procedure
who disappeared when the town was overrun in July 1995
wildflowers in a field
wristwatch to measure the hours
write this down

"*x*" has entered into the interior of the other person's seeing, entered there in
    the object of perception
x to mark the location where you were found
x stitched along the torn seam
XY karyotype drawn from marrow
examine every photograph and possession
exhaustion to overcome
exist in the book of memory
exist in the rain, berries, stones, and the night

you are here
you are not forgotten
you are this one and none other
you come to me in a dream
you keep asking
you lifted phosphorescence from the sea in strings of light
you scattered seeds
you were my ground

zenith bright above the earth where you were found
zero drift of loss
zinc selenium manganese cobalt iron
zippered jacket to hold in warmth
zona pellucida gathering light as the embryo forms
zone of memory
zone of the missing
zone of the night

Notes

I.

"Karyotype": A karyotype is the characteristic chromosome complement of a species; there are twenty-three paired chromosomes in the human karyotype. The word *karyotype* also refers to the iconic arrangement of these paired chromosomes in a black and white photograph. The italicized phrase on page 4 is from John Bostock's translation of *The Natural History of Pliny*, 1855. These poems were inspired by a National Geographic special that documented the attempt to extract intact DNA from the bone and tissue of several mummies found in the Tarim Basin, including the Beauty of Loulan. Elizabeth Wayland Barber's *The Mummies of Ürümchi*, which includes meticulous descriptions of their textile culture, is also intimately woven into this sequence.

II.

"On the ordering of chaotic bodies of poetry": The title of this poem and the details on Callimachus are taken from W. R. Johnson's *The Idea of Lyric: Lyric Modes in Ancient and Modern Poetry*. Johnson writes, with regard to Aristophanes of Byzantium's arrangement of the Pindaric corpus into seventeen books: "Beyond [Aristophanes'] immediate purpose—the ordering of chaotic bodies of poetry, the making of intelligible, enjoyable collections—the method he devised and refined had and continues to have major importance for the theory and practice of the lyric genre." The phrase "the idyllic era of cushions" is from Nadezhda Mandelstam's *Hope Against Hope*. Liu Baiqiang, a Chinese democracy activist, was sentenced in June 1989 to a further eight years of imprisonment for "counter-revolutionary incitement" and "propaganda," according to Amnesty International. He was released in the Fall of 2001.

"The semantic fields of glass and other transparent materials in the poetry of Krzysztof Kamil Baczyński": The epigraph is from his poem, "*Biała Magia*" ("White Magic"), translated by Bill Johnson in *White Magic and Other*

Poems. The title is an adaptation of an observation by Madeline G. Levine in *Contemporary Polish Poetry 1925–1975.*

"Field notes: Arras 1917": The British poet Edward Thomas enlisted in the Artists' Rifles in July 1915. He arrived in France in January 1917 and served with No. 244 siege battery. As noted in the archival description of his pocket diary quoted in "On the ordering of chaotic bodies of poetry," he was killed in April 1917 during the Battle of Arras. The italicized passage is from his daughter Myfanwy Thomas in her memoir of her father, *One of These Fine Days.*

"Russian notebook: Moscow 1918–1920": The epigraph, as well as most of the details in this poem, come from *Earthly Signs: Moscow Diaries 1917–1922.* The passage from the letter to Pasternak is from *The Same Solitude: Boris Pasternak and Marina Tsvetaeva*

"Russian notebook: Voronezh 1935–1937": Details of this period come from Nadezhda Mandelstam, *Hope Against Hope* and *Hope Abandoned,* and from the introduction to *The Voronezh Notebooks* (translators Richard and Elizabeth McKane) by Victor Krivulin. The italicized passage in the voice of the agronomist is from *Hope Against Hope.* The phrase "genre of silence" is from Isaak Babel, as quoted in Donald Rayfield's introduction to *Osip Mandelshtam: Selected Poems* (Penguin); the quotation on the Armenian language is also found in this introduction. Mandelstam's "namesake" was the Moscow physicist Leonid Isaakovich Mandelstam. He is known for his discovery of the combinatorial scattering of light.

"'In the long hours of darkness, Baghdad shakes to the constant low rumble of B-52s'": This title is the headline of an article written by Robert Fisk for *The Independent,* 26 March 2003.

"Poem from a burnt notebook": The epigraph is from Judith Hemschemeyer's translation in *The Complete Poems of Anna Akhmatova.* "This beautiful and mournful ritual" is from *The Akhmatova Journals* by Lydia Chukovskaya.

"Ash": The fall of burning pages after the firebombing of the National University Library of Bosnia and Herzegovina is described in an essay by Kemal Bakaršić, first published in *The New Combat*, Autumn 1994.

III.

Details on the Beauty of Loulan, Cherchen Man, the "Blue-eyed boy" and the Qäwrighul Child, as well as diagrams of tomb 85QZM2 ("Lines on a Cherchen Grave") are found in Elizabeth Wayland Barber's *The Mummies of Ürümchi* and J. P. Mallory and Victor Mair's *The Tarim Mummies*.

"Tokharian love song": It is believed that the Beauty of Loulan and her people may have spoken the now-extinct language of Tokharian, as many documents written in this language have been discovered in the Tarim Basin. Tokharian bears a relation to the Indo-European languages spoken in Europe and the Near East, such as English, Latin, Greek, Persian, and Sanskrit. Of the many documents written in Tokharian, only one poem has ever been found. My version is based on a literal translation of this poem in Mallory and Mair's *The Tarim Mummies*.

IV.

"Nothing is lost": The epigraphs are from Elaine Scarry, *The Body in Pain: The Making and Unmaking of the World*, and an ICRC news release found at http://www.icrc.org/eng/resources/documents/misc/57jr4h.htm. The phrase "cleaned and dried in the sun" is from Coroner's Report on Corpse No. 12, exhumed from a mass grave in the village of Abda, Hungary, at the end of the Second World War, cited in the introduction to *Under Gemini*, a selection of the poetry and prose of Miklós Radnóti. "We shall never meet again in this world" is from Anna Akhmatova's poem "In a Dream," part of the cycle "Sweetbriar in Blossom," translated by Elaine Feinstein in *Anna of All the Russias*.

Acknowledgements

My sincere thanks to the editors of the journals where some of these poems first appeared: *Grain, Contemporary Verse 2, The Antigonish Review, Existere, Event, Qwerty, The Fiddlehead, The Malahat Review,* and *Prairie Fire.* "Russian notebook: Voronezh 1935–1937" was awarded Second Place in *The Antigonish Review*'s 2012 Great Blue Heron Poetry Contest. "Cradle song: Six variations" won *The Fiddlehead*'s 22nd Annual Ralph Gustafson Poetry Prize. "Nothing is lost" was a co-winner of the 2013 *Malahat Review* Long Poem Prize and appeared in *The Best Canadian Poetry in English 2014.*

To Sylvia Legris for her generous encouragement of my work while she was editor of *Grain.*

To my editor Don McKay, for his close reading of *Karyotype* and many inspired suggestions, including those for the final ordering of the manuscript.

To everyone at Brick—Kitty, Barry, Alayna, Nick, Sue, and Marijke—who helped make this book.

And to my small band of humans.

KIM TRAINOR began writing poetry in the spring of 2009. Over the years she has worked at a campus radio station, the Department of Fisheries and Oceans, a biomedical library, and is currently a sessional lecturer at UBC. Her poetry has won *The Fiddlehead*'s Ralph Gustafson Prize and *The Malahat Review* Long Poem Prize, and has also appeared in the 2013 *Global Poetry Anthology* and *The Best Canadian Poetry in English 2014*. She lives in Vancouver.